WINNING CHESS FOR BEGINNERS

BY FRED REINFELD

(Originally published under the title *Chess Victory—Move by Move*)

PLAYER-VIEW™ PICTORIAL ILLUSTRATIONS ©1959
by WERNER SCHMIDT

GROSSET & DUNLAP • Publishers • New York
A National General Company

1973 Printing by Grosset & Dunlap, Inc.

ISBN: 0-448-02471-3 (Trade Edition)

Printed in the United States of America.

Preface to this New Printing

In the summer of 1972, two formidable International Grandmasters confronted each other across a chessboard in Reykjavik, Iceland, taking part in a competition that would determine anew the acknowledged chess champion of the world. At one end of the 64-square battlefield sat Boris Spassky, the Russian titleholder, successor to other Soviet grandmasters who had reigned supreme over all international challengers since 1937. Opposite him sat the American "superstar," 29-year-old Bobby Fischer, whose ascendancy in the ranks of the chess elite had been nothing short of phenomenal ever since his introduction to the game at the early age of six.

The match, which ultimately lasted two months and logged twenty-one games, at the outset was not expected to generate anything more than routine reportage and interest on the American side of the Atlantic, and then limited for the most part only to the most rabid of chess aficionados. But such expectations, most surprisingly, were to be surpassed by far. As the games continued apace, the mounting "score" in points seemed to take on a broad significance generally reserved for such popular events as a World Series. The moves and positions of the two contestants, represented by the black and white pieces on the chessboard, were duly set forth and analyzed in newspapers and periodicals, and studied by readers. Television viewers, some of whom did not know the rudimentary moves and objectives of the game, nevertheless strayed from standard programs to watch play-by-play recreations of the moves made in Iceland, as shown on Public Television Network stations. At one point, when these proceedings were interrupted by a switch to live coverage of a political National Committee meeting in Washington, irate callers swamped the TV-station switchboard with protests and forced a return to the chess play.

The 1972 world chess championship was terminated when Bobby Fischer defeated his opponent by gaining the required total points for victory and thus declared to be the new champion. With the sole exception of Paul Morphy, an outstanding player who dominated the chess scene more than a century ago (before the official world championship was actually designated), Fischer today is the only American to be recognized as best of all grandmasters.

The Bobby Fischer success story could not have come about so soon were it not for this young player's obvious total dedication to the game and his relentless pursuit of combinations that bring a winning advantage. Yet it is probably equally valid to credit his early introduction to the chessmen as a plus factor. This book, geared as it is for the beginner (and, indeed, even the "pre-beginner") in chess, will provide all the details needed to get started at playing the game, and playing it well. Here will be found, in simple, lucid text combined with a unique, innovative type of illustration, the basic moves, the basic checkmates, and a few elementary, yet ingenious, traps to avoid—or to spring on an unwary opponent—as familiar positions develop. You are likely to be pleasantly amazed and gratified at how readily you can grasp the fundamentals for victory from the move-by-move examples given.

Onward, now—and happy checkmate!

Contents

How to Use This Book

The key to studying and enjoying this book lies in the unusually large number of diagrams. For your reading pleasure a totally new kind of illustrative diagram has been devised, with figures that are much nearer "the real thing" than any diagrams used previously.

Every single move that actually occurs in play in this book is pictured on a diagram. Thus you can follow the changing situations from move to move in successive diagrams. It is literally true that you can get a complete grasp of what is happening, and why it happens, without taking the time to set up the pieces on a chessboard.

Note that after the first diagram in each sequence, the move or capture made is indicated by an arrow which starts at the square from which the piece moves, and extends to the square on which the move ended or a capture took place.

To get the most benefit out of the many brilliant and effective checkmates which make up this book, you will find it an excellent idea to cover up succeeding diagrams with a card. This will give you an opportunity to find the winning move yourself. Even in those cases where you fail to discover the best line of play, you will benefit just the same because you will get useful practice that will make you a better player. Wherever possible, try to study the play with a friend, because the exchange of ideas adds to the fun and stimulates your ingenuity.

Before You Begin

Perhaps you already know the elements of chess. If so, fine. In any case, here's a quick summary of what you need to know about the game:

Chess is played on a chessboard, with eight horizontal rows and eight vertical rows of eight squares each. All 64 squares are used.

Each player has 16 chessmen, as follows:

WHITE   BLACK

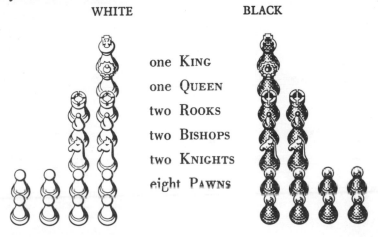

one KING

one QUEEN

two ROOKS

two BISHOPS

two KNIGHTS

eight PAWNS

White always moves first, and the board is so placed that the nearest corner square at his right is a white square.

The King can move in any direction, one square at a time.

The Queen can move vertically, horizontally or diagonally along the whole length of any line available to her. Friendly pieces block her path; enemy pieces on these lines can be captured by her.

THE OPENING POSITION

Note the rule of "Queen on color" in the opening position: White Queen on a white square, Black Queen on a black square.

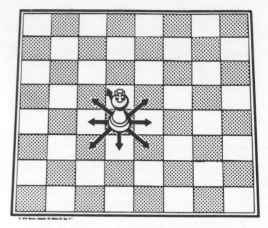

HOW THE KING MOVES

The King can move to any square indicated by a cross. The King captures in the same way.

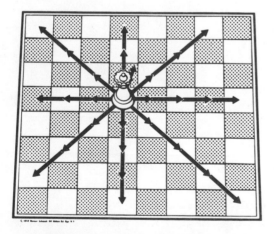

HOW THE QUEEN MOVES

The Queen can move to any square indicated by an arrow. The Queen can capture vertically, horizontally or diagonally.

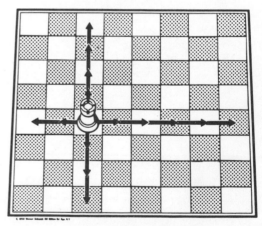

HOW THE ROOK MOVES

The Rook can move to any square indicated by an arrow. The Rook can capture vertically or horizontally.

14

The Rook can move horizontally or vertically.

The Bishop moves diagonally, one direction at a time.

The Knight is the only piece that can leap over other units. Its move is always of the same length: it moves one square up or down, and then two squares to the right or left; or one square to the right or left, and two squares up or down. It can capture hostile pieces only at the terminal square of its move.

The King, Queen, Rook, Bishop and Knight all capture the way they move,

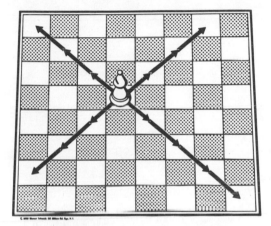

HOW THE BISHOP MOVES

The Bishop can move to any of the squares indicated by an arrow. The Bishop captures in the same way.

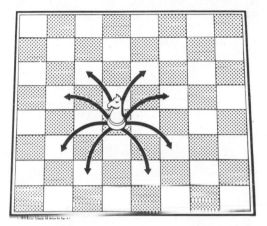

HOW THE KNIGHT MOVES

The Knight can move to any of the squares indicated by a cross. The Knight captures in the same way.

The Pawn has some curious properties. It can only move forward, one square at a time, except that the first time it moves, it can advance two squares. In capturing, however, it captures diagonally forward on an adjacent square.

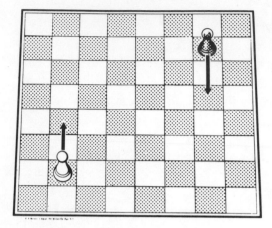

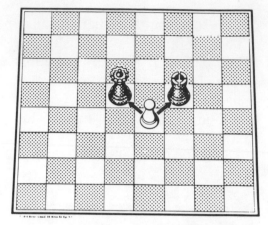

HOW THE PAWN MOVES

HOW THE PAWN CAPTURES

Each Pawn has the option of advancing one *or* two squares from the opening position.

The Pawn can capture the Queen *or* Rook.

The most important power of the Pawn is that when it reaches the last row, you can promote it to a new Queen, Rook, Bishop or Knight. In almost all cases the new piece is a Queen—for this is the strongest of all the pieces.

Basically, the way to win a game of chess is to attack ("check") the hostile King in such a way that no matter what your opponent does, he cannot get

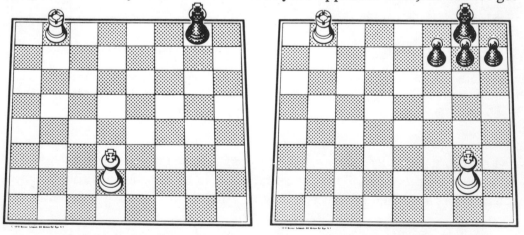

BLACK IS IN CHECK

BLACK IS CHECKMATED

out of the capturing range of one of your units. This is known as "checkmate." (A King can *never move into check*.)

A prospective loser does not always wait for checkmate. If he has lost too much material, he knows checkmate is inevitable, and so he resigns. If on the other hand there is not enough material to force checkmate, the game is given up as a draw, with honors even.

In order to get the King into a safe position, it is advisable to "castle" as early as possible. This can be done with the King and King Rook when there are no pieces between them. Move the King next to the Rook, and then place the Rook on the other side of the King, as shown below.

It is also possible to castle on the Queen-side with the Queen Rook when there are no pieces between the King and the Queen Rook. In that case the King moves two squares in the direction of the Queen Rook, which is then placed at the other side of the King.

QUEEN-SIDE CASTLING   KING-SIDE CASTLING

To derive the maximum value of this book, there are two features that you will very likely want to review quickly. One is to check up on the relative value of the chessmen. Expressed in points, their values are as follows:

VALUES OF THE PIECES

Queen	9 points
Rook	5 points
Bishop	3 points
Knight	3 points
Pawn	1 point

It is important to be absolutely certain of these values, for most games are decided by superiority in force.

Bishops (3 points) and Knights (3 points) are equal in value, but experienced players tend to favor the Bishop against the Knight.

A Bishop or Knight (3 points) is worth about three Pawns (3 points). If you give up a Knight and get three Pawns in return, you may consider it as more or less an even exchange. If you lose a Knight (3 points) for only a Pawn (1 point), you have lost material and should lose the game (if you are playing against an expert).

If you capture a Rook (5 points) for a Bishop or Knight (3 points), you are said to have "won the Exchange." If you lose a Rook (5 points) for a Bishop or Knight (3 points), you have "lost the Exchange."

The other important feature in reading a chess book is to be familiar with the chess notation. The following diagram shows how the squares are named from each side of the board:

QR8 (QR1)	QN8 (QN1)	QB8 (QB1)	Q8 (Q1)	K8 (K1)	KB8 (KB1)	KN8 (KN1)	KR8 (KR1)
QR7 (QR2)	QN7 (QN2)	QB7 (QB2)	Q7 (Q2)	K7 (K2)	KB7 (KB2)	KN7 (KN2)	KR7 (KR2)
QR6 (QR3)	QN6 (QN3)	QB6 (QB3)	Q6 (Q3)	K6 (K3)	KB6 (KB3)	KN6 (KN3)	KR6 (KR3)
QR5 (QR4)	QN5 (QN4)	QB5 (QB4)	Q5 (Q4)	K5 (K4)	KB5 (KB4)	KN5 (KN4)	KR5 (KR4)
QR4 (QR5)	QN4 (QN5)	QB4 (QB5)	Q4 (Q5)	K4 (K5)	KB4 (KB5)	KN4 (KN5)	KR4 (KR5)
QR3 (QR6)	QN3 (QN6)	QB3 (QB6)	Q3 (Q6)	K3 (K6)	KB3 (KB6)	KN3 (KN6)	KR3 (KR6)
QR2 (QR7)	QN2 (QN7)	QB2 (QB7)	Q2 (Q7)	K2 (K7)	KB2 (KB7)	KN2 (KN7)	KR2 (KR7)
QR1 (QR8)	QN1 (QN8)	QB1 (QB8)	Q1 (Q8)	K1 (K8)	KB1 (KB8)	KN1 (KN8)	KR1 (KR8)

WHITE

In recording White's moves, the White name of the square is used. In recording Black's moves, the Black name of the square is used.

At the beginning of the game, the King is placed at King 1 (K1). The Queen is placed at Queen 1 (Q1). The Bishops are placed at King Bishop 1 (KB1) and Queen Bishop 1 (QB1). The Knights are placed at King Knight1 (KN1) and Queen Knight 1 (QN1). The Rooks are placed at King Rook 1 (KR1) and Queen Rook 1 (QR1).

All the chessmen mentioned thus far go on the horizontal row nearest the player. The Pawns go on the next horizontal row—at King Rook 2 (KR2), King Knight 2 (KN2), King Bishop 2 (KB2), King 2 (K2), Queen 2 (Q2), Queen Bishop 2 (QB2), Queen Knight 2 (QN2) and Queen Rook 2 (QR2).

Although the special treatment of games and examples in this book makes only slight demands on your knowledge of chess notation, I advise you to master the notation thoroughly; it will open the gates to a lifetime of reading pleasure.

The following are the chief abbreviations used in the chess notation:

King—K	check—ch
Queen—Q	discovered check—dis ch
Rook—R	double check—dbl ch
Bishop—B	en passant—e.p.
Knight—N	good move—!
Pawn—P	very good move—!!
captures—x	bad move—?
to— —	very bad move—??

Here are some examples of abbreviations: N—KB3 means, "Knight moves to King Bishop 3." QxB means, "Queen captures Bishop." R—K8ch means, "Rook moves to King 8 giving check."

1. The Basic Checkmates

SUPERIOR FORCE MUST WIN

If you expect to win most of your games, it is essential for you to know the basic checkmates. For only when you are armed with this knowledge will you be certain of turning any material advantage into a win.

Your study of these checkmates has another value: it will familiarize you with the powers of each piece; and it will teach you how to make the pieces work together.

(White to play)

MATE WITH THE QUEEN

The Queen is the most powerful of all the chess pieces. This means that it is easier to force checkmate with the Queen than with other forces. But a word of caution is necessary: inexperienced players are so impressed with the Queen's power that they waste time giving useless checks. The best way is to try to cut down the number of squares the opposing King can move to. Like this:

To win by checkmating Black, you must drive the Black King to one of the four side rows of the board.

Why? Because when the King is on one of these rows he has less opportunity to move. For example: a King in the center has a choice of 8 moves. On a side row he has a choice of only 5 moves; in a corner square, he has even less choice—3 moves.

Once you force the King to a side square, you can easily prevent his escape. You will soon see how to place the Queen to cut off the Black King's escape.

Finally, your King must directly face the Black King with one square between them. Then you are ready to deliver checkmate.

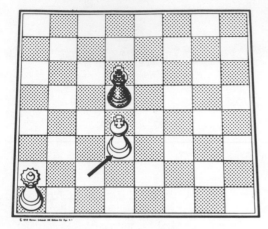

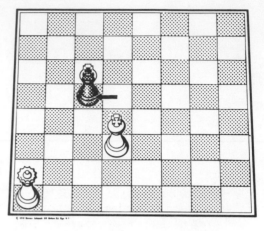

White plays **1 K—Q3** to reduce the number of squares to which Black's King can move. Only by cutting down the Black King's sphere of action can you *force* him to a side row, where he will be helpless.

Black plays **1 ... K—B4.** Of course he is unhappy about moving toward a side row, but whatever he plays causes him to lose ground in one way or another. For example, if he moves to the third rank, White's King advances.

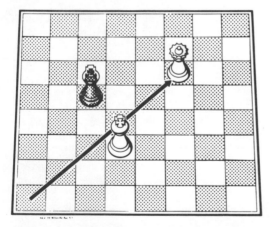

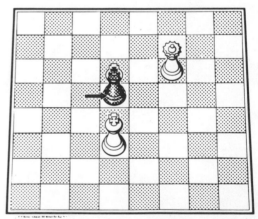

White plays **2 Q—B6.** The Queen gives a typical display of her power, darting out to cut off the Black King from three squares to which he might have been able to move.

Black plays **2 ... K—Q4.** As you can see, he is trying to keep his King in the center as long as he can, away from the fatal side squares. But White will drive him back.

22

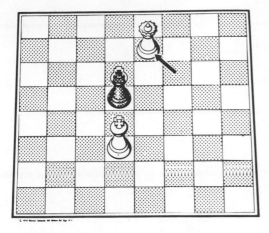

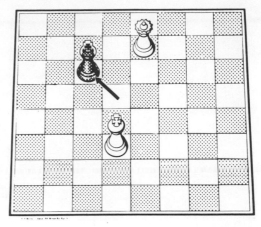

White plays **3 Q—K7,** leaving Black only one square to move to. It is interesting to note that White achieves more with "quiet" moves than he would with checks.

Black plays **3 ... K—B3.** He is doing the best he can to stay away from the side squares, but his efforts are hopeless if White knows his business.

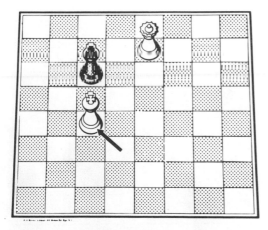

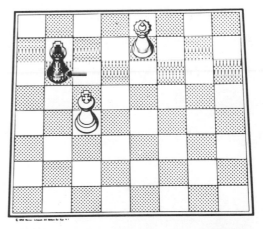

White plays **4 K—B4.** This is an important move, because it shows you that the White King must cooperate to bring about the coming checkmate.

Black plays **4 ... K—N3.** Again his King has only this one move. This harsh limitation on the Black King's moves tells us that he cannot hold out much longer.

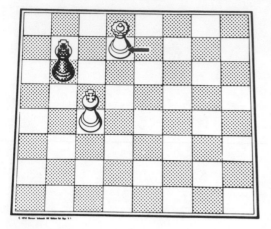

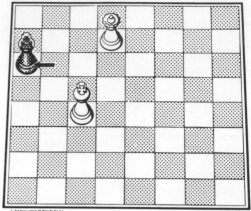

White plays **5 Q—Q7,** still continuing his policy of cutting down the Black King's moves. In fact, you can observe that Black's King *must* now go to a side square.

Black plays **5 ... K—R3.** He hopes that White will thoughtlessly reply 6 Q—QB7？？ This would stalemate the Black King, which, as you know, would give Black a draw.

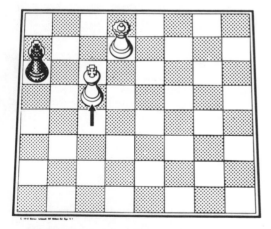

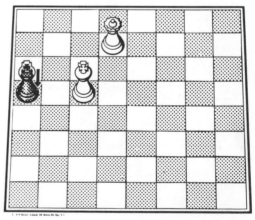

White plays **6 K—B5,** carefully avoiding the stalemate danger. Here is an important lesson for you: be doubly watchful when you are just on the point of winning a won game.

Black plays **6 ... K—R4.** Now that his stalemate try has failed, he is helpless against the coming checkmate. White has two ways of achieving his goal: 7 Q—QR7 mate or 7 Q—N5 mate.

24

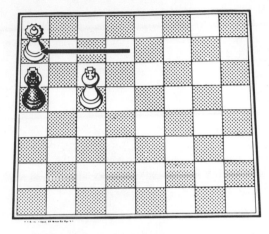

White plays **7 Q—QR7 mate.** Trapped on a side square, Black's King has no escape hatch. You can see why the close cooperation of White's King made the checkmate possible.

The powerful Queen, with her ability to move vertically, horizontally and diagonally, has made it fairly easy for the stronger White forces to checkmate Black.

You have seen that this process involves the following steps:

(a) advancing your King;

(b) placing your Queen (and King) in a position to cut off the hostile King from as many squares as possible;

(c) forcing the opposing King to a side row; and

(d) placing your King directly opposing the hostile King.

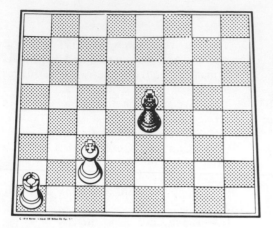

(White to play)

MATE WITH THE ROOK

To checkmate with the Rook, you follow pretty much the same procedure. However, you must bear in mind that the Rook lacks the Queen's power to make diagonal moves. Hence the Rook is a much weaker piece, and the checkmating process necessarily takes longer.

To reach the checkmate position, you must still force the hostile King to a side square. Then you must maneuver your King to face the other King directly. Finally you can give checkmate with a Rook check from which there is no escape.

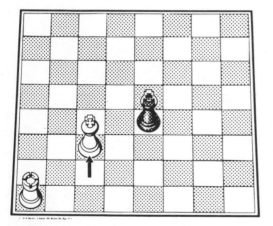

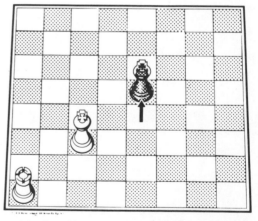

White plays **1 K—B3,** beginning the process of cutting down the possible moves that can be made by Black's King. If Black now plays 1 ... K—K6, White's reply would be 2 R—K1ch, forcing Black's King toward the side.

Black plays **1 ... K—K4,** craftily staying in the center—his best chance to stave off the process of being forced to a side row. White keeps advancing his King in order to force Black's King back.

26

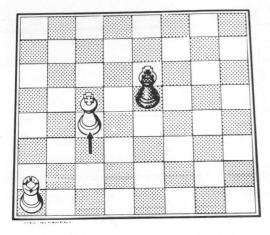

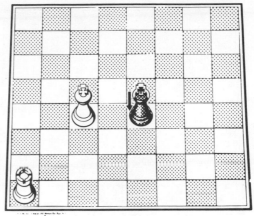

White plays **2 K—B4!** Now Black is in trouble. If he plays 2 ... K—B4, White replies 3 R—K1! cutting Black's King off from half the board. On the other hand, if the Black King retreats to the third rank, White replies 3 R—R5! with even more powerful effect.

Black plays **2 ... K—K5.** In this way he avoids the unfavorable lines you have examined in the previous note. Pay special attention to the position now reached: with *the Kings directly opposing each other*, the right continuation is a Rook check that forces the hostile King toward the side.

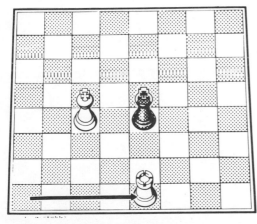

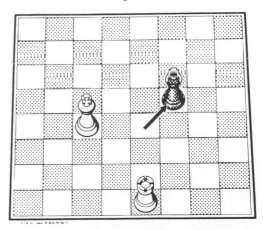

White plays **3 R—K1ch!**, the key to the ending. Thanks to the blockading position of White's King, Black is prevented from moving to the Queen file; instead, whether he likes it or not, he must retreat to the King Bishop file.

Black plays **3 ... K—B4**—one file nearer to the side.

Now it would be foolish for White to play 4 R—KB1ch, as Black would simply come back to the King file. So another White King move is in order.

27

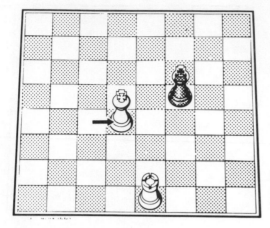

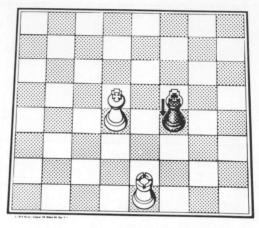

White plays **4 K—Q4,** once more creating an unpleasant situation for Black. If the Black King retreats to his third rank, the reply 5 R—K5! cuts him off from more territory.

Black plays **4 . . . K—B5,** trying to stand his ground. But now we have the same situation as after Black's second move: the two Kings face each other. How would you proceed in this situation?

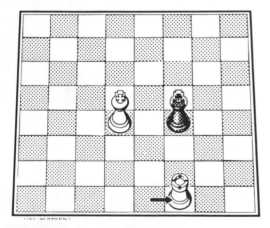

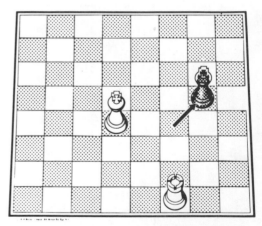

White plays **5 R—KB1ch!**—the typical Rook check which forces Black's King to the side because the White King blocks his approach.

Black plays **5 . . . K—N4,** one file nearer to the side. So far White has cut off Black's King from six files. Black is being hemmed in more and more.

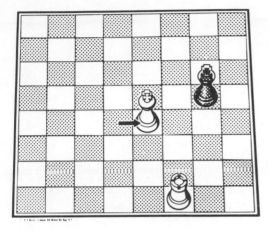

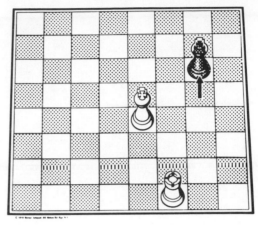

White plays **6 K—K4,** still pitilessly clos-
ing in on the Black King. In the event Black
tries 6 . . . K—N5, White replies 7 R—
KN1ch—the typical Rook check which
would finally drive Black to the side row.

Black plays **6 . . . K—N3**—still squirming.
Now White cannot make progress with a
Rook check. So once more he brings his
King a little closer. Sooner or later Black
will have to give way.

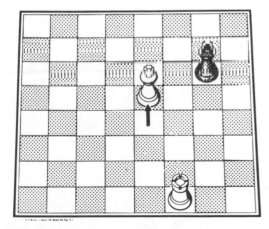

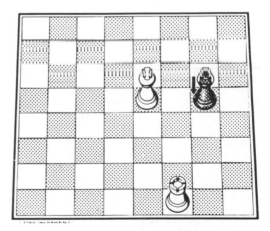

White plays **7 K—K5.** Now Black is
caught in a cleft stick, because if he retreats
(7 . . . K—N2), he is backing off toward a
side row. So he must try his luck in another
direction.

Black plays **7 . . . K—N4,** producing
another typical situation with which you are
thoroughly familiar by now; the two Kings
face each other. So again a Rook check is
in order.

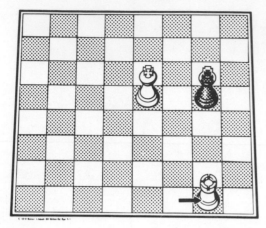

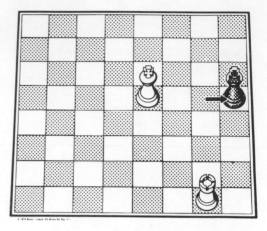

White plays **8 R—KN1ch.** At last he succeeds in his ambition to drive Black's King to a side row.

Black plays **8 . . . K—R4.** It does not matter which square the Black King moves to. White soon forces him into checkmate.

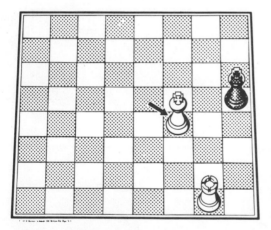

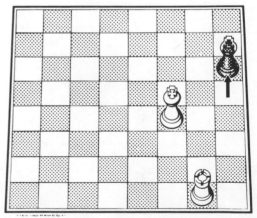

White plays **9 K—B4,** starting a deadly game of hide-and-seek with the Black King. Black cannot now play 9 . . . K—R5 because White can respond 10 R—KR1 mate.

Black plays **9 . . . K—R3,** steering clear of the standard checkmating position into which White is bent on forcing him. But now White repeats the maneuver.

30

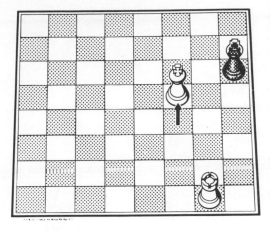

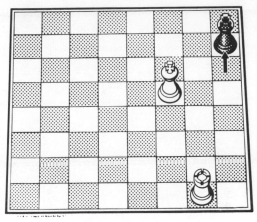

White plays **10 K—B5.** Now Black must not play 10 . . . K—R4 (allowing the Kings to face each other), for then White replies 11 R—KR1 mate.

Black plays **10 . . . K—R2,** retreating from the threat of checkmate. But, as you will soon see, time is running out for him.

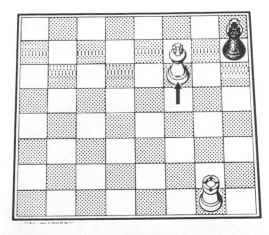

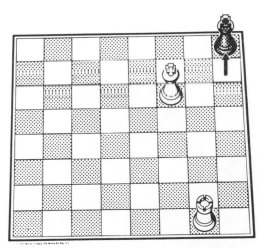

White plays **11 K—B6,** still stubbornly sticking to the same idea: if Black tries 11 . . . K—R3, White replies 12 R—KR1 mate.

Black plays **11 . . . K—R1,** momentarily escaping from checkmate. But since he is now in a corner square, he cannot retreat any further.

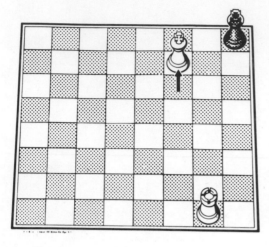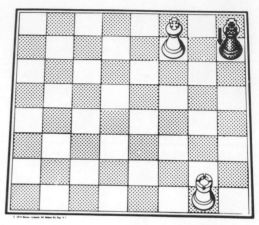

White plays **12 K—B7,** and now Black no longer has a choice: he *must* move his King into the fatal facing position.

Black plays **12 ... K—R2,** and now at last White has reached his goal. The time has come for the final Rook check.

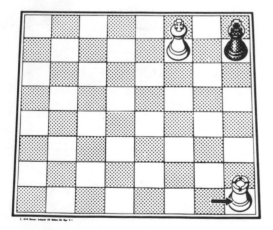

White plays **13 R—KR1 mate.**

In this final position you again see the pattern which first turned up on 3 R—K1ch.

Whenever the two Kings face each other with only one square between them, as we have observed repeatedly, a Rook check drives the lone King back.

To achieve the checkmate position, you must produce the very same situation, with the hostile King on a side row. Once the King has been driven to such a row, he has no escape—his further retreat has been cut off.

To checkmate with the Rook, then, you must:

(a) concentrate on driving back the hostile King;

(b) advance your King to deprive the opposing King of escape squares;

(c) check with your Rook at the right time.

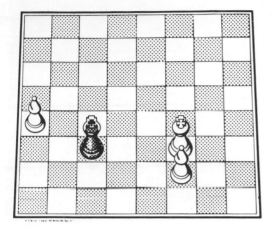

(White to play)

MATE WITH TWO BISHOPS

As you know, the Bishop is confined to squares of one color or the other as it moves diagonally only. As a result, a King and one Bishop cannot checkmate the hostile King.

However, you *can* force checkmate with King and both Bishops, for in that case you are able to command all 64 squares of the board.

To force the opposing King to the side of the board, as in the previous examples, is not enough. In this case, you can only checkmate after forcing the lone King into a corner square.

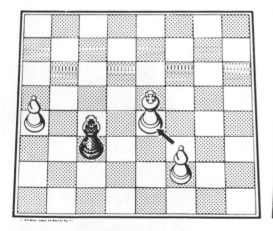

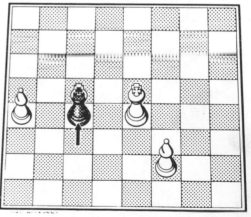

White plays **1 K—K4.** Black's King, as you know from earlier examples, can stave off checkmate only by heading for the center squares. Hence White's King must lend a hand in driving him back.

Black plays **1 ... K—B5.** White's first move prevented Black from playing ... K—Q6, and now, whether he likes it or not, his King will slowly be forced back toward the side of the board.

33

White plays **2 B—Q4!**, a typical and thematic move in this ending. The black-squared Bishop operates in two directions, thus depriving Black's King of two useful moves.

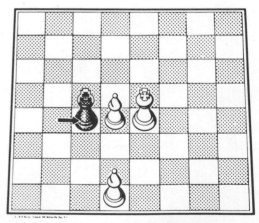

Black plays **2 ... K—N5.** Thanks to White's last move, he cannot play ... K—B4 or ... K—B6. The result is that he is forced toward the side of the board.

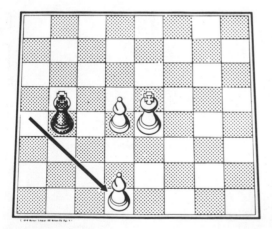

White plays **3 B—Q1**, retreating his attacked Bishop. The lull is only temporary. He will soon force the pace again.

Black plays **3 ... K—B5.** Watch now how neatly White forces him away from this square and nudges him toward the side.

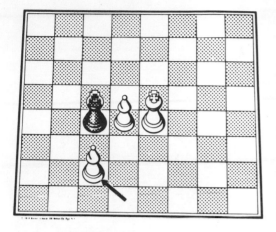

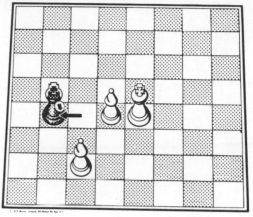

White plays **4 B—QB2.** This quiet little move is not so harmless as it looks. Black's King must go toward the side now, and White gets the opportunity to seize valuable space.

Black plays **4 . . . K—N5**—unwillingly, to be sure. But now White takes an important step forward; can you see how? Remember, the idea is to deprive Black's King of possible moves.

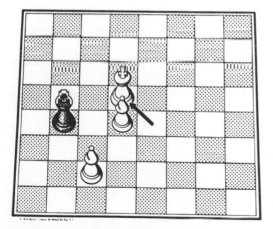

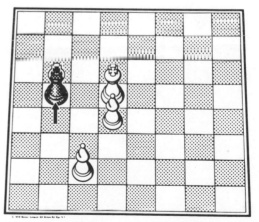

White plays **5 K—Q5.** Now Black can never play . . . K—B5. Obviously the area left for Black's King is shrinking.

Black plays **5 . . . K—N4.** Slowly but surely White is pushing the Black King to the wall.

35

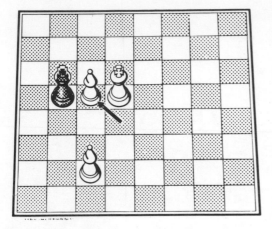

White plays **6 B—QB5!** Like White's second move, this prevents the Black King from moving up or down. Black must give way again.

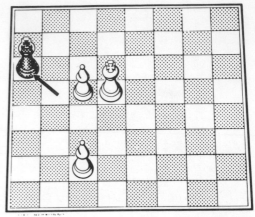

Black plays **6 ... K—R3.** White's clever maneuvering has forced Black's King to the side. The next step is to force him into the corner.

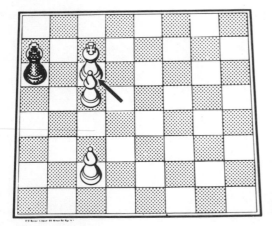

White plays **7 K—B6.** This prevents the Black King from running away by means of ... K—N2 etc.

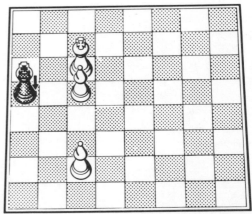

Black plays **7 ... K—R4.** His King tries to inch away from the corner square, but he cannot get very far.

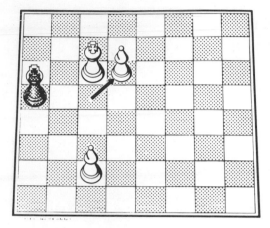

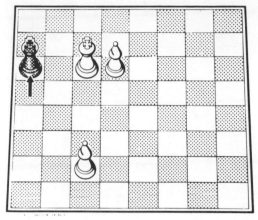

White plays **8 B—Q6,** marking time until he can play B—N4. Notice this quiet procedure and the avoidance of flashy checks which would only waste time.

Black plays **8 . . . K—R3.** If he expects to continue swinging his King back and forth from Queen Rook 3 to Queen Rook 4, he soon discovers how wrong he is.

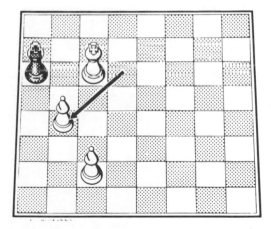

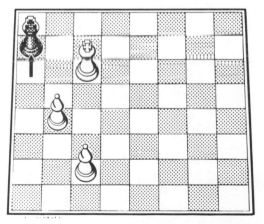

Now White plays **9 B—N4,** which rules out . . . K—R4. Thus the Black King is herded toward the corner.

Black plays **9 . . . K—R2.** This forced approach to the corner is the beginning of the end. Now White's King takes a hand again.

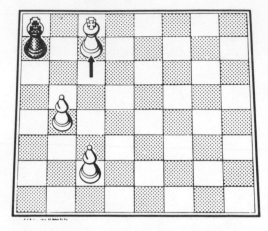

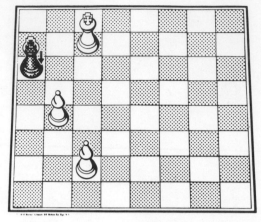

White plays **10 K—B7.** As you will see in the coming checkmating sequence, this move is necessary to prevent the King from escaping out of the corner and also to clear a diagonal for an important check.

Black plays **10 ... K—R3.** After this, White forces checkmate in three moves. But 10 ... K—R1 is no better, as the play would go: 11 B—Q3, K—R2; 12 B—B5ch, K—R1; 13 B—K4 mate.

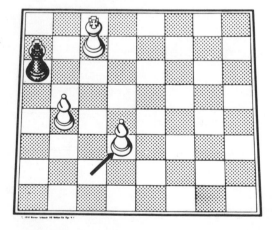

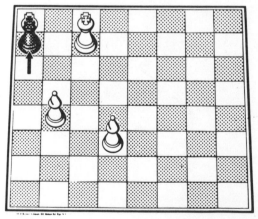

White plays **11 B—Q3ch.** Now that the decisive stage has arrived, checks are in order.

Black plays **11 ... K—R2.** Note the magnificent cooperation of the two Bishops in bringing about checkmate.

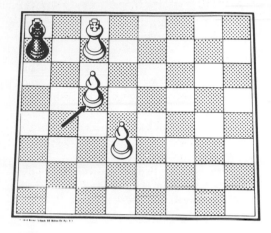

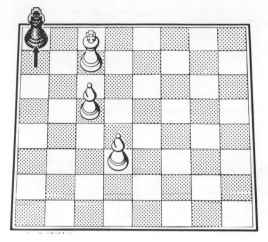

White plays **12 B—QB5ch.** Now you can see why it was necessary to force the Black King into a corner.

Black plays **12 ... K—R1.** With the Black King's moves reduced to zero, White is able to checkmate on the move.

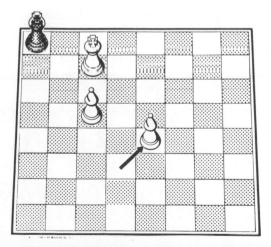

White plays **13 B—K4 mate.**

Checkmate with the two Bishops, as you can see, makes a wonderful study because it requires delicate cooperation by the checkmating forces.

A vital point that you must not underestimate is the importance of the stronger side's King. Only by steadily advancing your King can you cut down the moves of the opposing King and thus gradually drive him into the corner checkmate situation.

As in the case of the other checkmates, you must drill yourself repeatedly in this procedure until you have mastered it thoroughly.

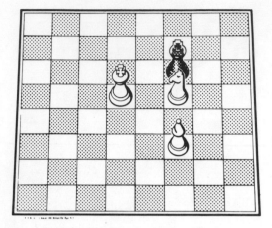

(White to play)

MATE WITH BISHOP AND KNIGHT

This is the most difficult of all the basic checkmates, and you must study it very carefully.

You can only bring this checkmate about on a corner square which is of the same color as those covered by your one Bishop; in this case, White's King Rook 1 or Queen Rook 8. You will find that there must be the closest kind of cooperation among the checkmating pieces.

In this case the Bishop controls the white squares, while the King and Knight must primarily control the *black* squares.

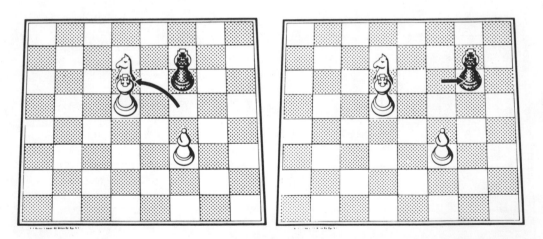

White plays **1 N—Q6.** The first phase: to force Black's King away from the center to one of the four outside rows.

Black plays **1 . . . K—N3.** As long as he can do so, he heads away from either of the *white* corner squares.

40

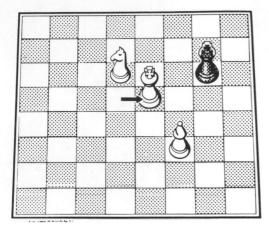

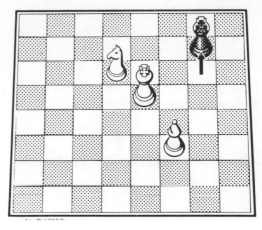

White plays **2 K—K5.** Thus he deprives Black of the opportunity to play . . . K—B3 again.

Black plays **2 . . . K—N2.** If he tries 2 . . . K—N4, the reply N—B7ch drives his King back.

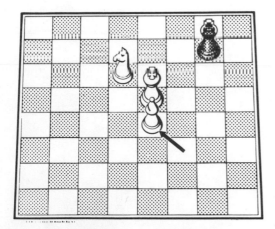

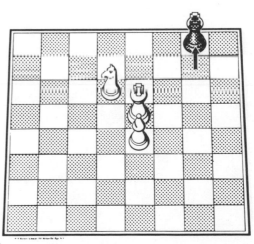

White plays **3 B—K4,** preventing . . . K—N3. This move forces Black's King to the side or end of the board. But the play that follows calls for a great deal of patience.

Black plays **3 . . . K—N1.** Note that . . . K—R3 would be no better, as White simply replies 4 K—B6 and Black's King is stranded on a side row with the same kind of play that now follows.

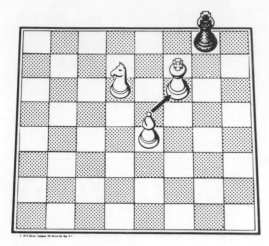

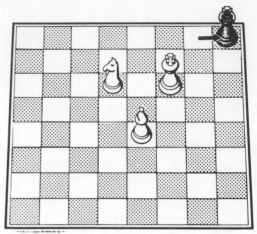

White plays **4 K—B6,** shutting the prison gates with a bang. (He prevents Black's escape by means of . . . K—N2.)

Black plays **4 . . . K—R1.** Heading away from the white corner, he says defiantly: "Come and get me!"

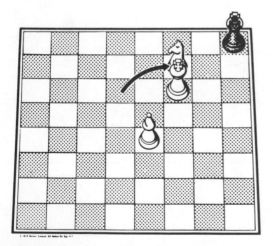

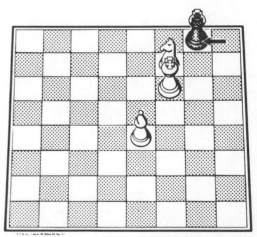

White plays **5 N—B7ch** starting the Black King on his unwilling journey to a white corner.

Black plays **5 . . . K—N1.** He gives ground only when he must. Now White must force him further to the left.

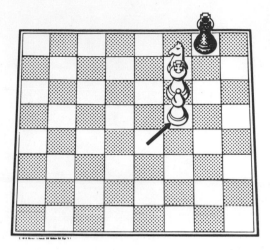

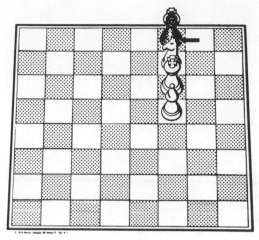

White plays 6 **B—B5**—a waiting move. He wants to play B—R7, but he cannot do this at once.

Black plays **6 . . . K—B1.** This forced move gives White the opportunity he is waiting for.

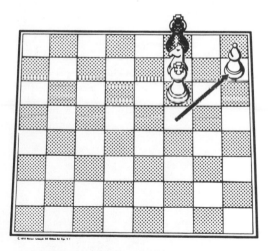

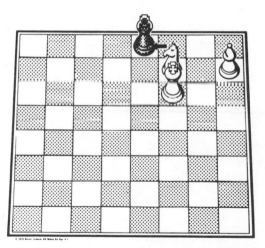

White plays **7 B—R7!** preventing . . . K—N1 and thus forcing Black's King toward the left white corner. Without such *systematic forcing moves*, this ending can offer endless difficulty. With them, the ending is fun.

Black plays **7 . . . K—K1.** You might think he is on the point of escaping to freedom with . . . K—Q2; it would take some hard work to get him back on the track again. But White is ready to block the exit and keep him on the back rank.

43

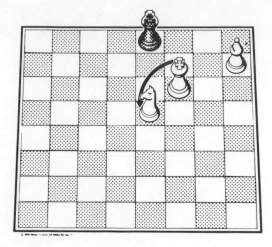

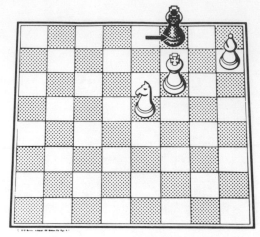

White plays **8 N—K5!** This effectively prevents Black's King from escaping by means of . . . K—Q2. Trying to escape by way of . . . K—Q1 would be futile, as we shall soon see.

Black plays **8 . . . K—B1.** If he tries 8 . . . K—Q1; 9 K—K6, K—B2 he is driven back with 10 B—B2!, K—N3; 11 K —Q6, K—R4; 12 K—B5 etc.

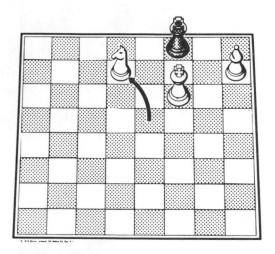

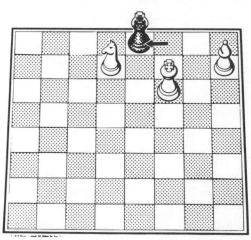

White plays **9 N—Q7ch,** once more forcing Black's King to head toward the white corner. Now the trip goes smoothly.

Black plays **9 . . . K—K1,** as retreat in the other direction is impossible. Now White keeps up the pressure.

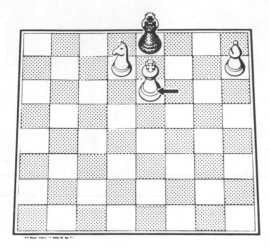

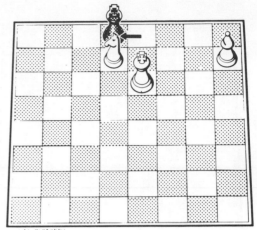

White plays **10 K—K6,** guarding his Knight and also making sure that his King cooperates in the checkmating process.

Black plays **10 . . . K—Q1.** Move by move, as you can see, White is forcing the Black King toward the white corner.

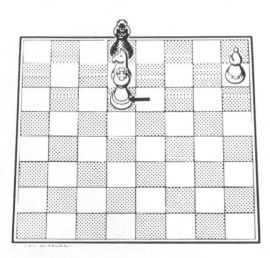

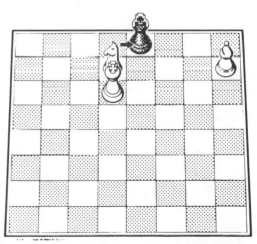

White plays **11 K—Q6.** In this way he prevents . . . K—B2 and keeps Black's King nailed to the back rank.

Black plays **11 . . . K—K1,** again threatening to escape from the back rank. But White is on his guard.

45

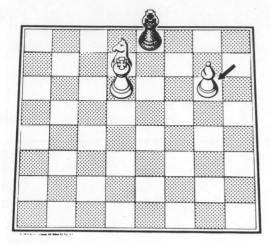

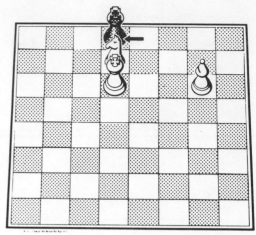

White plays **12 B—N6ch,** preventing the escape of the Black King and driving him in the desired direction.

Black plays **12 . . . K—Q1;** very sad, for on the next move too he will have to go again in the direction of the white corner.

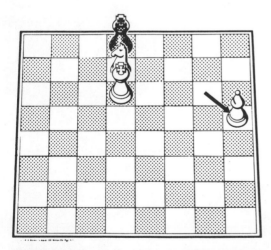

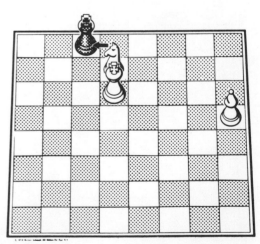

White plays **13 B—R5**—a waiting move. Note how White continues to control his King 8 with the Bishop, making it impossible for Black's King to flee. So White makes real headway.

Black plays **13 . . . K—B1.** The power of White's forcing moves gives you a good idea of the pleasure to be gained from chess when you get the most out of the chess pieces.

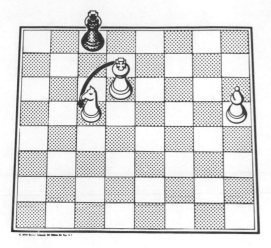

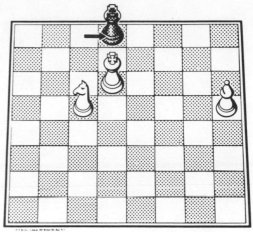

White plays **14 N—B5,** which you will recognize as an echo of 8 N—K5! This time he uses the same pattern to force the Black King into the white corner.

Black plays **14 . . . K—Q1.** Black realizes that if he plays 14 . . . K—N1 White replies 15 B—N4! after which the checkmate comes a bit sooner.

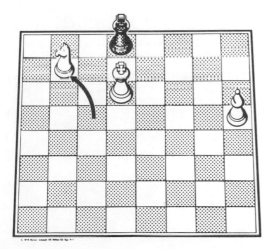

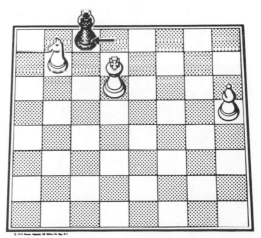

White plays **15 N—N7ch.** This check enables White to drive the Black King to Queen Knight 1 after all.

Black plays **15 . . . K—B1.** Even at this stage an inexperienced player might carelessly let Black's King slip out.

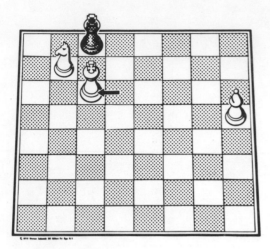

White plays **16 K—B6,** protecting his Knight and shifting to the neighborhood of the all-important corner square.

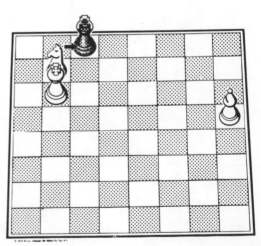

Black plays **16 ... K—N1,** hoping against hope for a dash to Queen Rook 2, which would delay matters a bit.

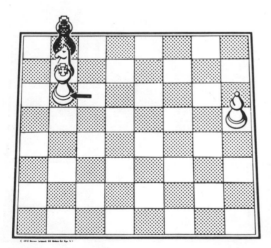

White plays **17 K—N6,** alertly blocking this attempt to escape. With the same move he has set the stage for checkmate—leaving open the long white diagonal for his Bishop to control.

Black plays **17 ... K—B1.** This is the last time he is able to wiggle away from the white corner.

48

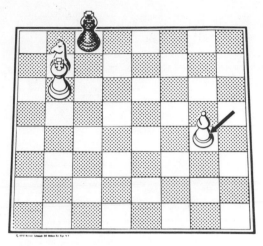

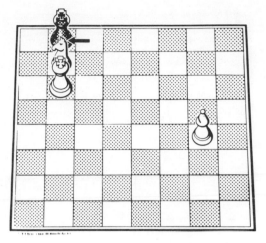

White plays **18 B—N4ch,** completing the pattern that drives the Black King toward the fatal corner.

Black plays **18 . . . K—N1.** Now White will checkmate in four more moves. Can you see how?

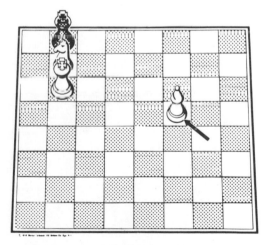

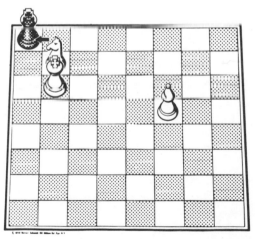

White plays **19 B—B5,** losing a move in order next to play N—B5 followed by N—R6ch. That is to say, he wants his Knight to come to Rook 6 with check. (If he plays 19 N—B5, K—R1; 20 N—R6?? Black is stalemated and escapes with a draw.)

Black plays **19 . . . K—R1.** Now that he is in the white corner, the mate will come quickly enough. Since White has lost a move, there is no danger of his having to concede a draw by carelessly running into a stalemate.

49

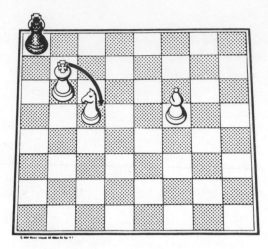

White plays **20 N—B5.** The purpose of this maneuver is to prevent the Black King's flight from the corner at the decisive stage.

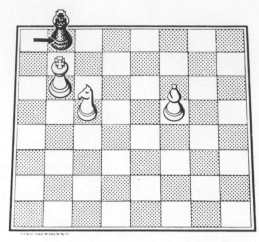

Black plays **20 . . . K—N1.** His King cannot escape. At this point you can appreciate all of White's finesse and foresight in driving the King here.

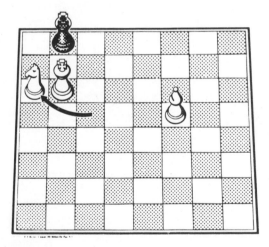

White plays **21 N—R6ch.** He is now ready to deliver checkmate on his next move.

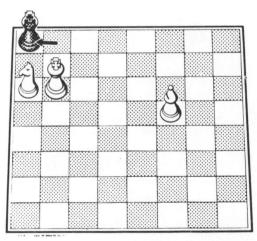

Black plays **21 . . . K—R1.** With his King boxed in, he is helpless against the coming mate.

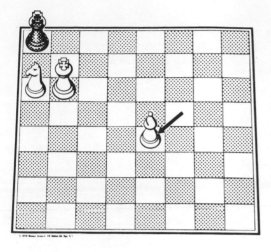

White plays **22 B—K4 mate.** Only the Bishop can give the final check in this ending.

The checkmate with Bishop and Knight, as you have seen, is the most difficult of the basic checkmates. But for just that very reason, it is the most rewarding. To bring about this checkmate, you have to combine the moves of King, Bishop and Knight carefully and patiently.

Another point about this ending is that it gives you useful practice in maneuvering with the Knight—the piece that causes the most trouble for inexperienced players.

2. Checkmate in Actual Play

To master the basic checkmates by repeated practice is fairly easy. But when you come to the task of recognizing checkmate possibilities in your games you may find yourself at a loss. Why is this? Because in actual play, the checkmate pattern is often hidden in what looks like a complicated position until you learn what to look for.

The first position pictured in each sequence in this chapter is the setting for a forced checkmate. Sometimes the checkmate is obvious; sometimes it is made up of delightful surprise moves.

What this all adds up to, as you will see, is a highly concentrated course in selecting *the elements that really matter* in each opening position.

TRIUMPH OF BLACK'S BISHOPS

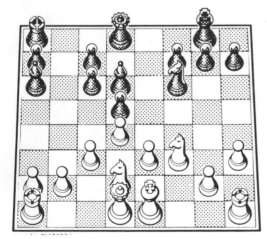

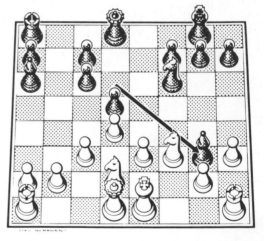

(Black to play)

Black's Bishops are all-powerful. The crossfire of their long, open diagonals converges on White's helpless and uncastled King. This King is a perfect target.

Black plays **1 ... B—N6 mate.** It is easy to appreciate the power of the checking Bishop, but the long-range effectiveness of the other Bishop is even more impressive.

52

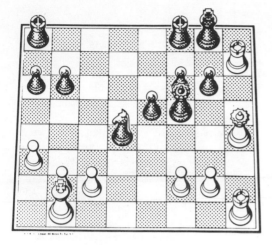

(White to play)

White forces checkmate in two moves.

THE OPEN FILE DECIDES

White is a piece down, but that is not the whole story. You can see that he has massed his forces threateningly on the open King Rook file. And, as you will soon find out, Black King is at the mercy of White's Queen and Rooks.

Yet when you start searching for the checkmate, it turns out not to be so easy to find. For example, if you try 1 R—R8ch, K—B2; 2 Q—R7ch Black has 2 . . . K—K1.

But there is a more forthright procedure. *You must hit hard!*

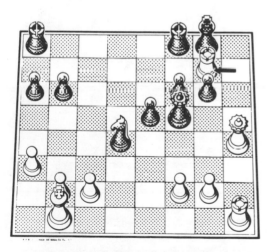

White plays **1 R—KN7ch!**—a devilish sacrifice which leaves Black no choice. *No choice*—remember that for future examples.

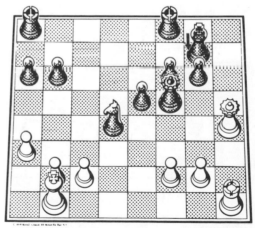

Black plays **1 . . . KxR.** Now White is a Rook and Knight down; but that doesn't matter because he has checkmate within his grasp. How so?

53

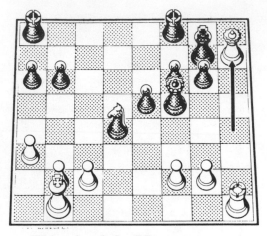

White plays **2 Q—R7 mate.**

You have learned something of priceless importance from this checkmating sequence. If you want to force checkmate, it is essential for you to seek powerful moves that leave your opponent no choice, or as little choice as possible.

When you make moves that leave your opponent ample freedom of action, you can take it for granted that an early checkmate is not in sight (unless he blunders).

Restraint and coercion—these are the trademarks of a checkmate attack. In this case, for example, 1 R—KN7ch! left Black no choice—a strong hint that White was on the right track.

BLACK MUST NOT TAKE A NEW QUEEN!

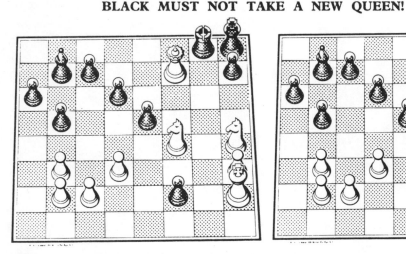

(Black to play)

Black forces checkmate on the move.

As matters stand, Black suffers from a serious minus in material. By queening his King Bishop Pawn, he can change the minus to a plus, but then he loses: 1 . . . P—B8/ Q??; 2 N/B4—N6ch, PxN; 3 QxQ and White wins.

Black plays **1 . . . P—B8/N mate!**

So you see that *not* asking for a Queen but "underpromoting" to a Knight is artistic and surprising—and also Black's strongest move! Black hits hard and gives his opponent no choice. The astounding move wins; the ordinary move loses.

54

WHITE MUST FIND A CRUSHING DOUBLE CHECK

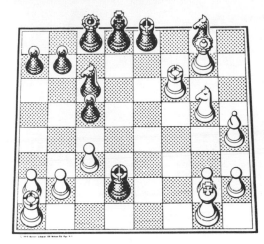

(White to play)

White forces checkmate in two moves.

A little study of this position shows you that White's win must depend on opening up the diagonal that leads from White's Bishop to Black's King. How you are to clear this diagonal is far from obvious.

Thus, 1 N—B7ch allows Black's King to escape.

To be sure, 1 N—K6ch is stronger, for then 1 ... RxN allows 2 R—B8 mate (a brutal *double check*). But after 1 N—K6ch Black can try 1 ... QxN, which loses quickly but nevertheless prevents an immediate mate.

What then is White's *most forcing* checkmate method?

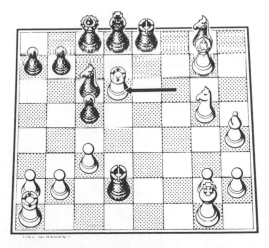

White plays **1 R—Q6ch!** This may look nonsensical, but you must admit that it is forcing.

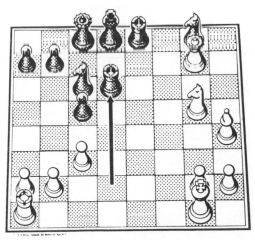

Black plays **1 ... RxR,** which is both obvious and unavoidable. But now the deadly diagonal can be cleared.

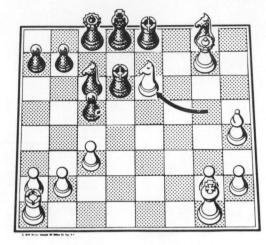

White plays **2 N—K6 mate.**

White's problem, you now realize, was to produce a setting for a *double check*. Once this becomes clear, the surprise 1 R—Q6ch! is no longer a surprise.

What makes the double check so hard to combat is that two pieces are giving check at the same time. This rules out interposing or capturing as a possible reply.

The only way to escape from a double check is to move the attacked King. When the King cannot move (which is the case here), the double check becomes checkmate.

LOOK FOR A DOUBLE CHECK

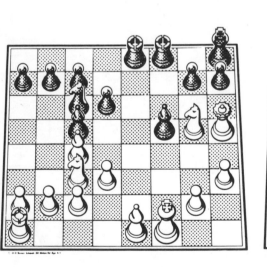

(Black to play)

Black checkmates on the move.

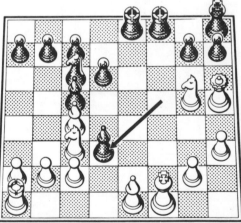

Black plays **1 ... BxQP mate.** White is helpless against this double check because his King has no move.

WHITE STARTS WITH A QUEEN SACRIFICE

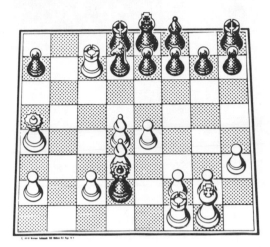

One look at this position discloses that White's pieces are very aggressively placed. As for Black, his Queen is badly out of play and most of his other pieces are undeveloped. His hemmed-in King is an obvious target.

This is all very well, but how would you proceed? How does White transform his undeniable advantage into a mate in three moves?

(*White to play*)
White forces checkmate in three moves.

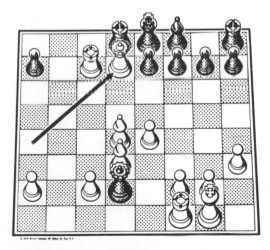

White plays **1 QxNch!** The Queen sacrifice is based on White's overwhelming lead in *active* development. Note that Black's reply is forced.

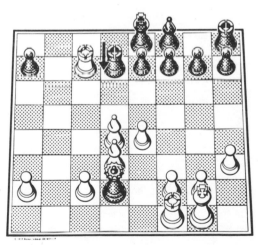

Black plays **1 ... RxQ.** He is helpless against the coming attack. Lack of effective defensive resources defeats him.

57

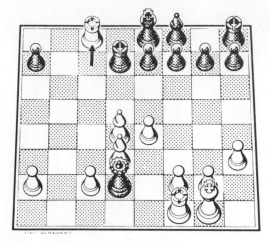

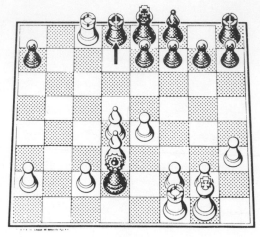

White plays **2 R—B8ch.** Again we see the element of force—Black has only one reply.

Black plays **2 ... R—Q1.** He has no defense to the coming Bishop check, which explains the Queen sacrifice.

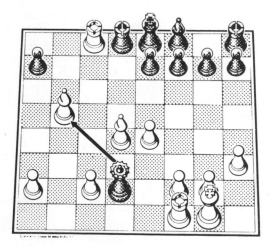

White's superior mobility assured the success of his attack. His margin of advantage was so great that the Black Queen might just as well not have been on the board.

To put it another way, White's superior mobility permitted him to make forcing moves—to dictate Black's replies. These are the factors that enable you to checkmate quickly.

White plays **3 B—N5 mate.** Black's pinned Rook cannot interpose.

58

WHITE MUST ELIMINATE BLACK'S QUEEN FROM THE DEFENSE

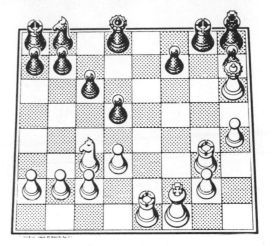

(White to play)

White has two *potential* mating threats. At the moment Black has adequate protection against both.

Thus, Black's Rook at King Knight 1 prevents Q—N7 mate. And Black's Queen stops Q—B6ch forcing mate.

Yet White has an extra Rook in play, as Black's Rook at Queen Rook 1 is useless. How can White put his advantage to good use?

White forces checkmate in three moves.

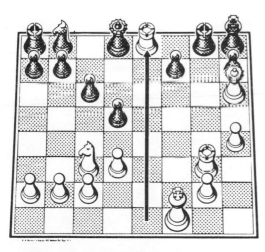

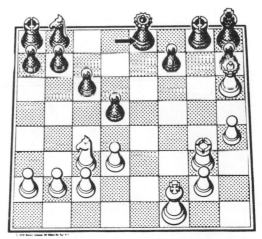

White plays **1 R—K8!!**

This brilliant surprise move threatens 2 Q—N7 mate or 2 R/N3xR mate.

Nor can Black play 1 . . . RxR because of 2 Q—N7 mate.

Black plays **1 . . . QxR,** restoring communication between his Queen and his Rook at King Knight 1.

Nevertheless, Black must lose. Can you see why?

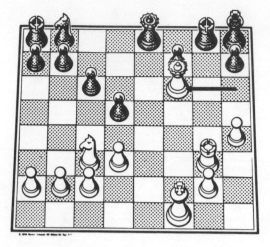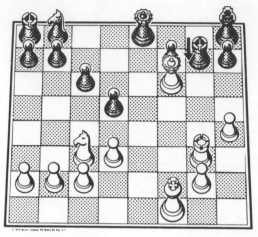

White plays **2 Q—B6ch.** This works now that Black's Queen is out of the way.

Black plays **2 . . . R—N2**—a forced reply. Now White is able to force mate on the move.

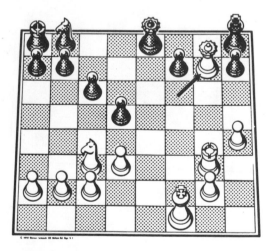

You have seen that this checkmating process clearly demonstrated the power of White's extra Rook in play. Black was simply outnumbered and overwhelmed.

Yet an even more basic factor had a strong influence on the play. Black's King was exposed to attack because his King Knight Pawn had disappeared earlier from his King Knight 2 square. Because of this, White's Queen was able to reach the powerful post King Rook 6, with results that you have seen.

White plays **3 QxR mate.**

BLACK'S KING IS BOXED IN

White is a Rook down. Ordinarily we would dismiss the position as hopelessly lost for him; but this is not an ordinary position.

The amazing fact is that White has deliberately played for this position, and that he can force checkmate in three moves. How can we explain this?

White has sacrificed *material* to gain *time*. If he can make every move tell, he can win before Black has a chance to use his material advantage.

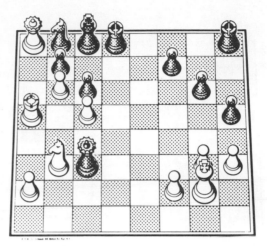

(*White to play*)

White forces checkmate in three moves.

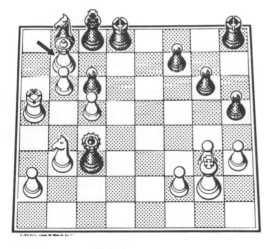

White plays **1 QxPch!!** There is method in his seeming madness.

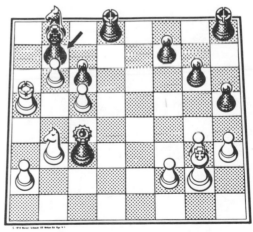

Black plays **1 . . . KxQ.** Surprised or not, he has to capture.

61

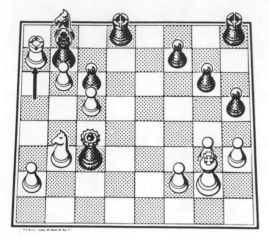

White plays **2 R—R7ch.** The approaching mate is taking on shape.

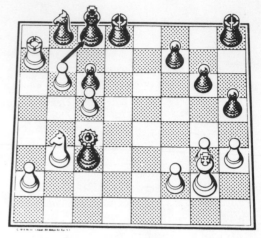

Black plays **2 ... K—B1.** His King can get no help.

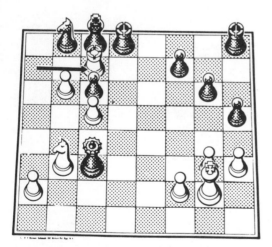

White plays **3 R—B7 mate.** The escape of Black's King is blocked by his own pieces!

White has forced checkmate by hitting hard and not giving Black a chance to catch his breath.

Black paid a heavy price by having his pieces posted where they were unable to exert any power or come to the aid of his King.

WHITE HAS AN ASTOUNDING QUEEN SACRIFICE

In this situation, most players with the White pieces would play QxQP. In that event, White would of course maintain the marked advantage he has with his command of the open King Rook file.

But the position offers much more to an imaginative player. By adopting dynamic forcing measures, White can bring off a quick checkmate.

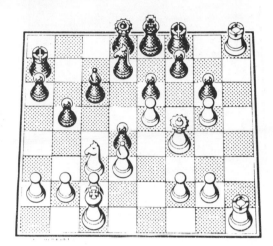

(*White to play*)

White forces checkmate in three moves.

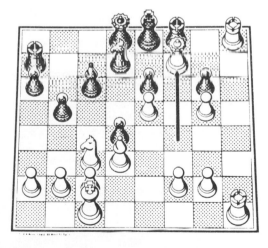

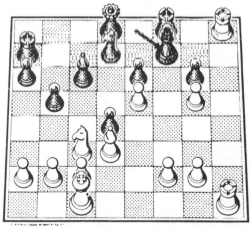

White plays **1 QxBPch!!** leaving Black no choice.

Black must play **1 ... KxQ.** How does White continue?

63

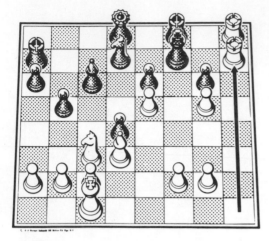

White plays **2 R/R1—R7ch** and again Black's reply is forced.

Black plays **2 ... K—K1.** Black's pieces are curiously helpless.

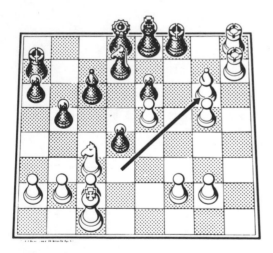

White plays **3 BxKNP mate.** Black's pinned Rook cannot interpose.

How was it possible for White to give up his Queen right in the heart of the enemy's camp and force a quick checkmate despite the presence of so many Black pieces in the vicinity?

The answer lies in White's powerfully efficient mobility. The open King Rook file was the road to victory.

White's advantage in mobility was so great that he was able to engineer a checkmate even after parting with his most important piece.

64

BLACK SETS UP A DECISIVE DOUBLE CHECK

To find a good move is sometimes not enough—there may be a better one. This position is a case in point.

Black has a winning game with . . . Q—K5ch. Ordinarily, there would be no point in looking further. But in this case, if Black looks sharply, he can force a brilliant mate.

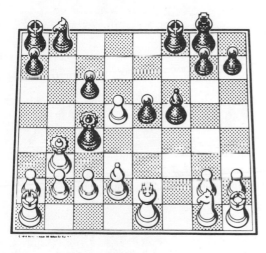

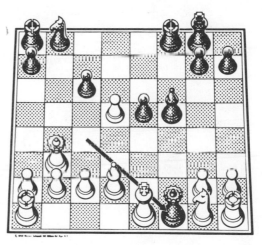

(*Black to play*)

Black forces checkmate in three moves.

To do this, he has to start the ball rolling with an unusually brilliant Queen sacrifice.

Black plays **1 . . . Q—B8ch!!** The underlying idea behind this move is that Black can make use of the open King Bishop file to force checkmate.

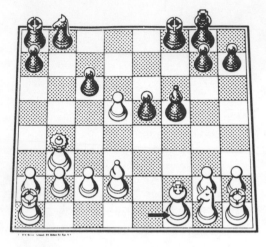 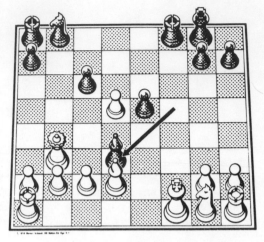

White plays **2 KxQ**—a forced move, of course.

Black plays **2 ... B—Q6 dbl ch.** The *double check* explains everything.

White plays **3 K—K1.** Now you can see that the whole point of Black's striking Queen sacrifice was to set up a *double check* and thus force the White King to walk into checkmate.

Black plays **3 ... R—B8 mate.** The way in which Black, through the double check, blocks off White's Queen from the defense is very pleasing. This increases our appreciation of Black's startling sacrifice.

66

BLACK WINS ON THE LONG DIAGONAL

White is a Rook ahead and in addition he threatens R—K8 mate on his next move.

True, Black has a few checks, but they don't amount to anything; for example 1 . . .QxPch; 2 K—B1; Q—R6ch; 3 K—B2 and White's King slips out easily.

Yet—if Black can find the right first move, he will force a quick checkmate. We know this will require the close cooperation of his Queen, his Bishop and his advanced Pawn at King Bishop 6. Can you see how Black achieves victory?

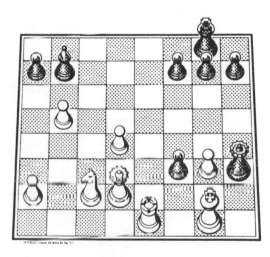 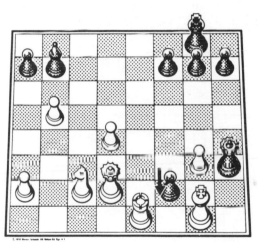

(Black to play)

Black forces checkmate in three moves. His first move is tantalizing.

Black plays **1 . . . P—B7ch!!**—not brilliant, but a hard-to-find move just the same.

67

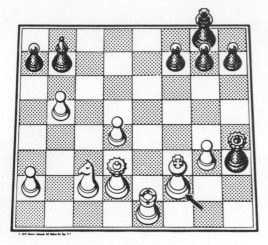

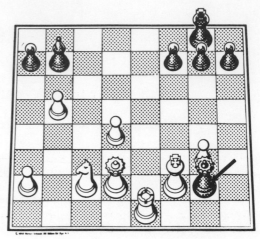

White plays **2 KxP** in the realization that 2 QxP allows . . . Q—R8 mate; a neat point.

Black plays **2 . . . Q—N7ch.** Now begins the cooperation of his Queen and Bishop on the long diagonal.

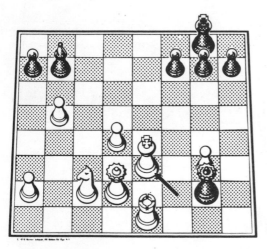

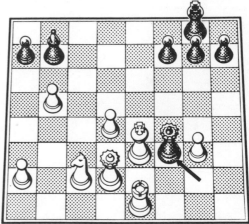

White plays **3 K—K3.** His extra material is really useless to him now.

Black plays **3 . . . Q—B6 mate.** Thus his 1 . . . P—B7ch!! has been vindicated.

68

FOR A QUICK WIN, WHITE'S QUEEN MUST JOIN THE ATTACK

White is a Rook down, yet his position is well worth it, for all his pieces are admirably posted for attack. Black's King has been stripped of his customary shield of King-side Pawns; Black's Queen is out of play, unable to take part in the defense.

If White plays uninspired chess he can win with 1 R—R3ch, K—N2; 2 Q—R5 etc. But he has a much more forcing win.

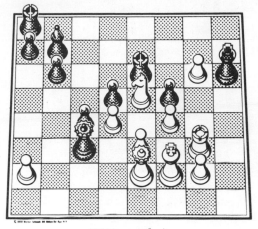

(*White to play*)

White forces checkmate in three moves.

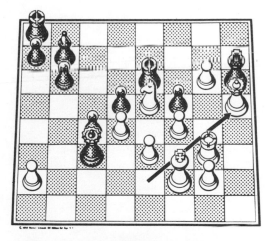

White plays **1 Q—R5ch!!**, a bombshell. If Black takes the unprotected Queen with his King, he succumbs to 2 R—R3 mate.

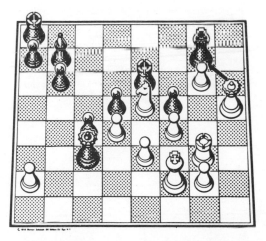

Black plays **1 ... K—N2**—forced, to avoid mate. But this relief is only temporary.

69

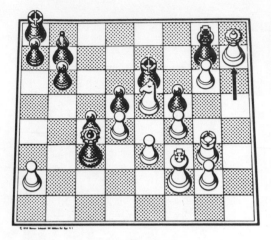

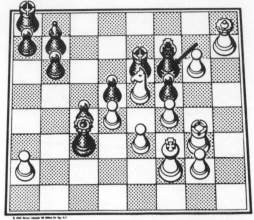

White plays **2 Q—R7ch.** Black's King, deprived of all supporting defense, has no chance.

Black plays **2 ... K—B3.** If he plays 2 ... K—B1 instead, White checkmates with the same reply.

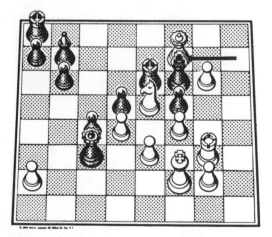

This is the kind of finish you can expect from positions in which a King is exposed to concentrated attack and has no defensive support from his own pieces.

White's pretty opening move 1 Q—R5ch!! is instructive as well as elegant. It gives you an idea of the brilliant possibilities presented to the attacking player when the defender's forces are scattered and useless.

White plays **3 Q—KB7 mate.**

70

BLACK'S SIMPLEST MOVE IS A QUEEN SACRIFICE!

White, with two Rooks against two minor pieces, is considerably ahead in material. Yet Black has a won game because of his powerful attacking position, not to mention his two connected passed Pawns.

Black can proceed in simple fashion or in an ingenious way. Curiously enough, the "simple" move leads to unwelcome complications, whereas the ingenious move batters down White's resistance. Let's think it out.

The "simple" move for Black is 1 . . . N—B3, retreating the attacked Knight. But then White plays 2 Q—B4, preventing 2 . . . P—K6 because White will reply 3 QxB and then White wins easily. If Black tries 2 . . . B—R2, White can reply 3 QxRP and suddenly White's Queen-side Pawns look very powerful.

Another obvious first move for Black is 1 . . . Q—N6 (threatening . . . Q—R7 mate). If White replies 2 PxN?? Black counters with 2 . . . Q—R5 mate. But if White has his wits about him he replies 2 Q—B5ch, keeping Black busy with a series of Queen checks.

All this is worrisome for Black—and quite unnecessary. For he has a dazzling Queen sacrifice which forces mate in three.

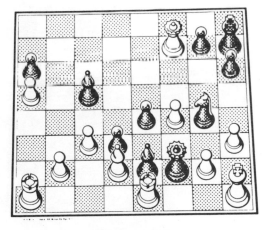

(*Black to play*)

Black forces checkmate in three moves.

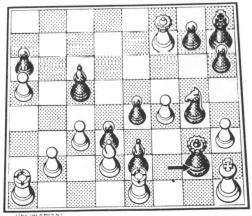

Black plays **1 . . . QxNPch!!**

71

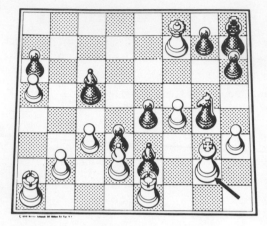

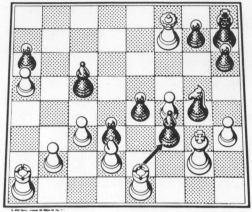

White plays **2 KxQ.** It seems unbelievable that Black can force checkmate relying only on his remaining minor pieces. Yet that is what happens.

Black plays **2 . . . B—B6ch.** In contrast to the puzzling complications described in the introduction, Black has no vexing alternatives to deal with here.

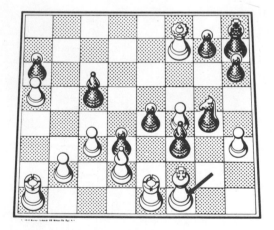

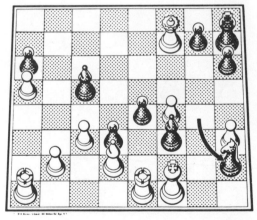

White plays **3 K—B1.** His helplessness is pathetic.

Black plays **3 . . . N—R7 mate.** A remarkably pretty combination.

BLACK WINS ON THE LONG DIAGONAL!

Black's overwhelming concentration of force on the King-side assures him of a win.
White's forces are huddled together without much rhyme or reason. Most ominous of all, his Queen is far from the scene of action.

Black can win eventually with the obvious 1 . . . RxN/Q7, but he has a much more forcing method. He sees that the mighty diagonal of his Queen Bishop is the key to a quick win.

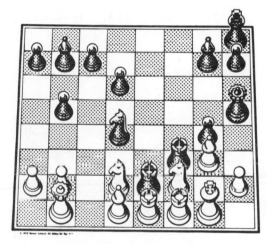

(*Black to play*)

Black forces checkmate in three moves.

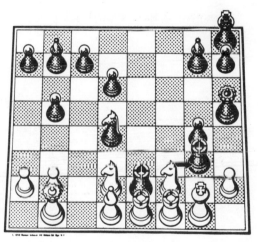

Black plays **1 . . . RxBch!**

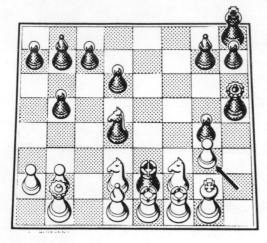

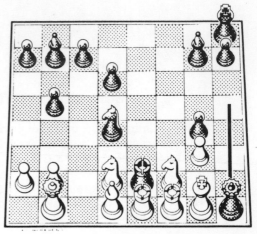

White plays **2 PxR.** Now Black is ready for another sacrifice.

Black plays **2 ... Q—R8ch!!,** sacrificing his Queen to achieve a checkmating position.

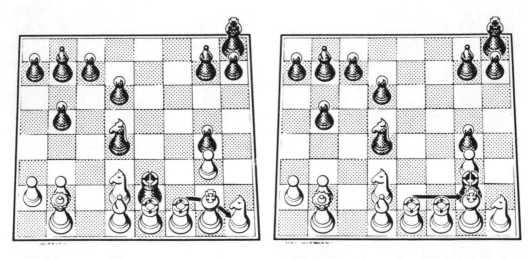

White plays **3 NxQ.** Do you see why Black played for the removal of this Knight from King Bishop 2?

Black plays **3 ... R—N7 mate.** He has successfully carried out the idea of attacking along the long diagonal, and White's King has been blocked by his own pieces.

74

WHITE MUST DRIVE BLACK'S QUEEN AWAY

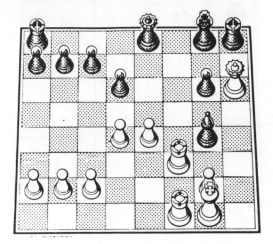

White is a piece down and seems about to lose more material: his Queen and one of his Rooks are attacked.

Yet there is no reason for White to despair. If he knows how to take advantage of the Black King's unfortunate position, he can bring about a neat checkmate.

(White to play)

White forces checkmate in three moves.

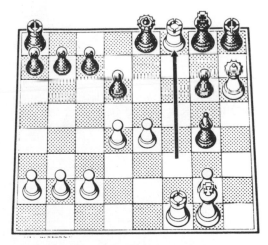

White plays **1 R—B8ch!** His main object is to strip Black's King Knight Pawn of its present protection.

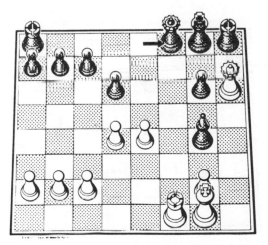

Black plays **1 ... QxR,** forced. Can you work out the checkmate pattern that White is aiming for?

75

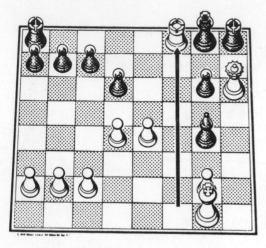 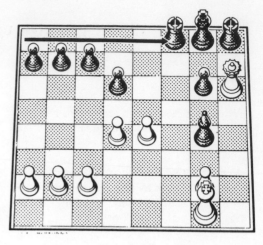

White plays **2 RxQch,** still forcing the issue.

Black plays **2 ... RxR.** His moves are dictated by White.

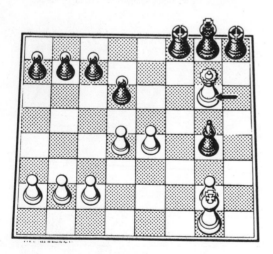

It took imagination for White to foresee that Black's King would be hemmed in by his own pieces and would therefore be helpless against the mating attack.

White plays **3 QxP mate!** A neat finish.

A DISCOVERED CHECK WINS FOR BLACK—BUT WHICH CHECK?

A puzzling position for Black. He has a powerful attack—his pieces are well placed and White's King is exposed to serious threats.

And yet it is not easy for Black to find the right continuation.

Thus, 1 . . . N—K5 dis ch looks murderous, but White replies 2 P—N3! attacking Black's Queen in turn and also threatening 3 RxR mate.

Being a piece down, Black must find a quickly decisive line of play.

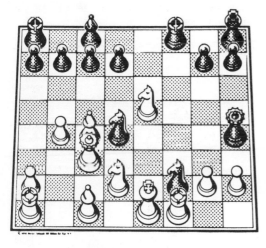

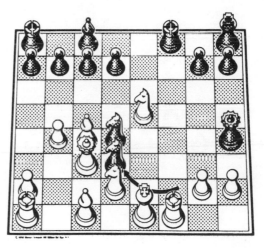

(*Black to play*)

Black forces checkmate in three moves.   Black plays **1 . . . N—Q6 dbl ch.**

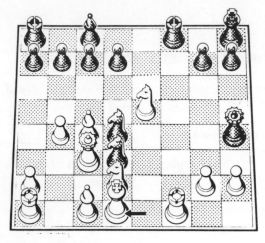

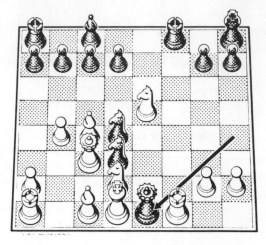

White plays **2 K—Q1,** still threatening RxR mate. Can you see any continuation that will keep Black's attack alive?

Black plays **2 . . . Q—K8ch!!** This brilliant sacrifice enables Black to bring off an amazing mate.

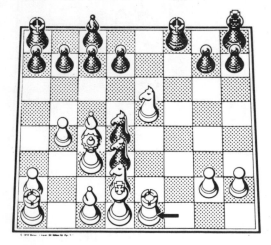

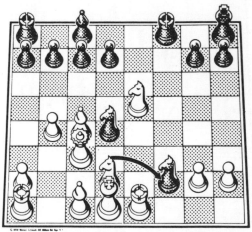

White plays **3 RxQ.** Now his King is hemmed in.

Black plays **3 . . . N—KB7 mate.** A re-markable "smothering" checkmate.

BLACK'S MINOR PIECES TRAP WHITE'S KING

Black has sacrificed a Rook for the attack. Therefore he must make every move tell.

His Queen is attacked, and so is his Knight at King 5. Yet Black can win with 1 . . . NxNch; 2 BxN, BxB threatening . . . Q—Q5 mate or . . . N—B4 mate.

This is clever enough to satisfy most players. But Black prefers a more direct—and more artistic—method.

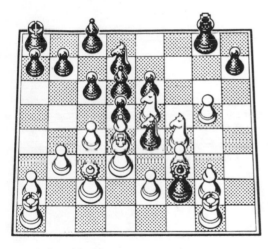

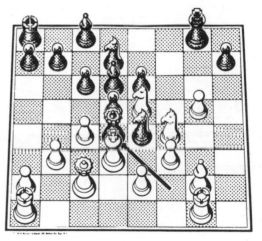

(*Black to play*)

Black forces checkmate in three moves.

Black plays **1 . . . QxBch!!**

79

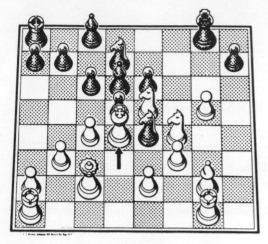

White plays **2 KxQ.** Note that now
2 . . . BxNch? allows White to escape.

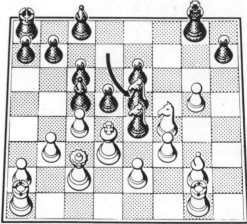

Black plays **2 . . . B—B4ch!**—the right
move to force mate.

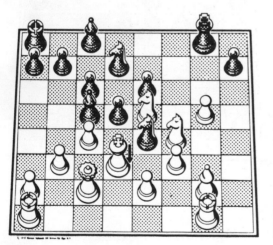

White plays **3 K—Q3.** It is curious that
his enormous material advantage does him
no good.

Black plays **3 . . . NxN mate.** An extra-
ordinary checkmate position. The White
King is pathetically helpless.

3. Early Checkmate Possibilities

In actual play the opportunities for quick checkmate are much commoner than most of us realize. Of course, such opportunities arise only because of serious blunders during the first few moves. But while the blunders occur frequently, the other player rarely takes advantage of them. In this concluding section we shall pinpoint some early mistakes and see how to pounce on them for a quick win.

Generally you will find that faulty or neglected development leads to the kind of position we are discussing. A player with a huge lead in development is bound to have a powerful position and this can often open up the lines for a quick checkmate. Sometimes an opponent's thoughtless slip exposes the target King to an immediately decisive break-through.

So much for preparation. When we come to the critical situation, we are ready to engineer a quick checkmate of the kind that we have been studying in the previous section. Since the mistakes shown in these games are typical, you will be able to take advantage of similar blunders when made by your opponents in your own games.

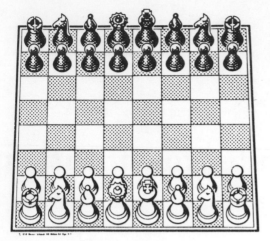

GAME 1

White	Black
Hamlisch	Amateur

Vienna, 1902

KING FIANCHETTO DEFENSE

White quickly obtains an overwhelming position with direct threats against Black's King. The result is that White checkmates after only seven moves.

White plays **1 P—K4,** taking up a strong position in the center and opening up lines for bringing out ("developing") his pieces.

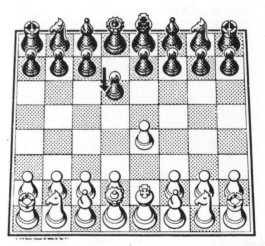

Black plays **1 ... P—Q3.** This gives him a cramped, passive position and contributes nothing to the development of his pieces.

82

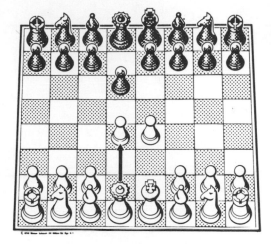

White plays **2 P—Q4.** This gives him a commanding position in the center. He expects to develop his pieces in a bold, sweeping manner. The initiative is his.

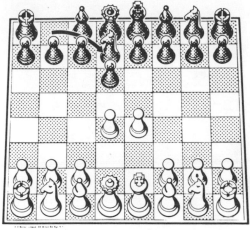

Black plays **2 ... N—Q2**—a timid move which leaves him a cramped, crowded position. Instead, 2 ... N—KB3 would have been more logical and would have gained time by attacking White's King Pawn.

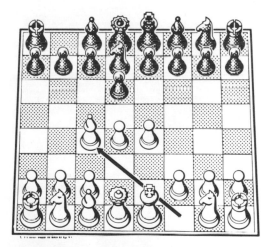

White plays **3 B—QB4**—an aggressive move that may involve the later threat of BxPch under favorable circumstances.

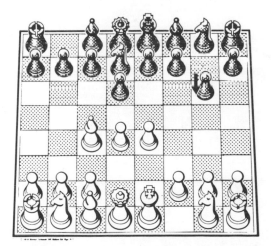

Black plays **3 ... P—KN3.** He is unconscious of any danger. He could have made better moves in 3 ... KN—B3 or ... P—K4.

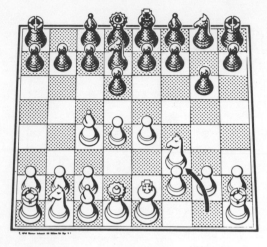

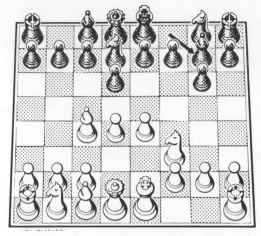

White plays **4 N—KB3,** developing another piece. He has a threat (do you see it?) which Black can parry with 4 . . . P—K3 or . . . N—N3.

Black plays **4 . . . B—N2?,** overlooking White's threat. Thus, with the game barely started, Black has already ruined his prospects of getting a good position.

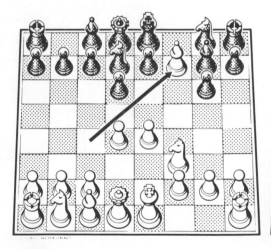

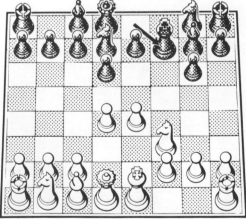

White plays **5 BxPch!**—a brilliant sacrifice best answered by . . . K—B1. (Even in that case White's material and positional advantage would be decisive.)

Black plays **5 . . . KxB?** He overlooks the full force of White's attack, which he can appreciate only after White's coming Knight check.

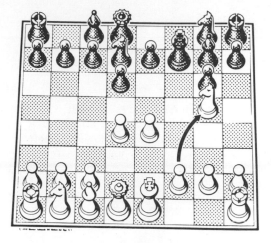

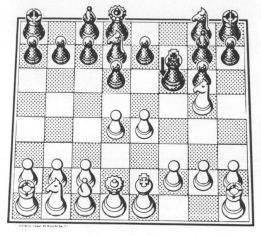

White plays **6 N—N5ch**—a move of unexpected power. Thus, if Black plays ... K—K1 or ... K—B1, White wins the Black Queen by playing his Knight to King 6.

Black plays **6 ... K—B3.** He saves his Queen, but only at the cost of allowing himself to be checkmated. However, his game was hopeless anyway, so this move is not exactly a blunder.

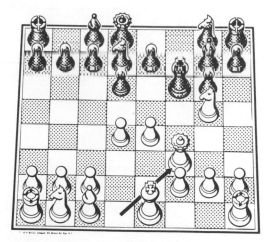

White plays **7 Q—B3 mate.**

This impressively brief game points out the dangers of failing to develop the pieces quickly and efficiently.

Black's slow development would have left him tied up in knots in any event. But as the game actually went, White's alert and forceful attack quickly provided the punishment that his opponent's timid play deserved.

When your opponent neglects the development of his pieces, you can often set up a quickly decisive attack against his helpless and exposed King.

85

GAME 2

White	Black
Damant	Amateur

London, 1932

CARO-KANN DEFENSE

Black wastes valuable time in this game with thoughtless Knight moves. The result, as you will see, is that White is able to start a vicious attack at an astonishingly early stage.

It takes White very little time to checkmate the Black King, which is helpless and hemmed in.

White plays **1 P—K4,** taking up a strong position in the center and immediately opening up lines for developing his pieces.

Black plays **1 . . . P—QB3.** He will follow this up with 2 . . . P—Q4, disputing White's control of the center by challenging White's King Pawn.

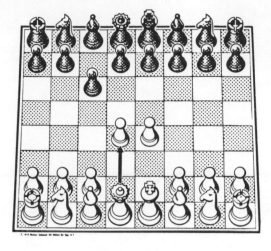

White plays **2 P—Q4.** This gives him a commanding position in the center. But this is only temporary if Black counters properly with 2 . . . P—Q4.

Black plays **2 . . . P—Q4.** He is fighting for his fair share of the center. He will have a good game after 3 PxP, PxP—or 4 P—K5, B—B4 etc.

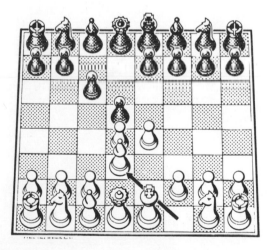

White plays **3 B—Q3** (actually 3 N—QB3 is preferable). Now Black can get a good game with 3 . . . PxP; 4 BxP, N—B3 gaining valuable time for development.

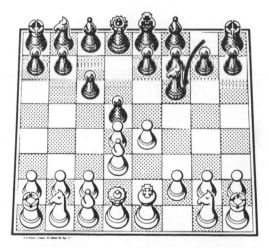

Black plays **3 . . . N—B3?** This is a developing move, to be sure, but bad at this moment. White will now obtain an overwhelming position by driving the Knight away.

87

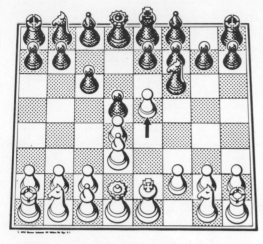

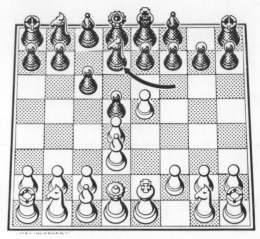

White plays **4 P—K5**—very powerful, for
4 . . . N—N1 leaves Black with a wretchedly
undeveloped game, while 4 . . . N—K5?;
5 P—KB3 costs Black a piece, as the Knight
would be lost.

Black plays **4 . . . KN—Q2.** Now his
pieces are in each other's way, and the out-
look for his future development is very poor.
Realizing that he has the initiative, White
forces the issue.

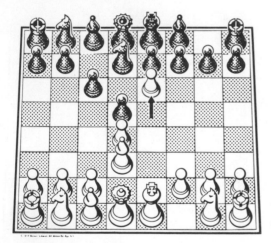

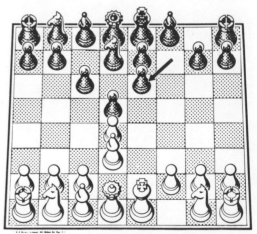

White plays **5 P—K6,** setting a devilish
trap. Black's best play now is 5 . . . N—B3;
6 PxPch, KxP even though his King loses
the castling privilege.

Black plays **5 . . . PxP??** He has succumb-
ed to the trap, overlooking the prospect of
the coming mating attack. White's reply
forces mate.

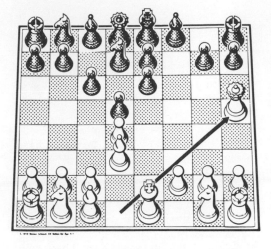

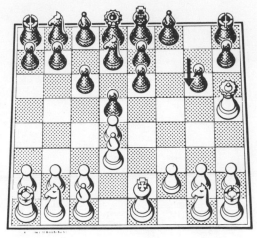

White plays **6 Q—R5ch.** Black's blundering capture has opened the gates to his enemy. Black's King gets no support from his other pieces.

Black plays **6 . . . P—KN3**—the only way to meet the check. His endangered King is hemmed in and has no escape. The Pawn interposition is no help either.

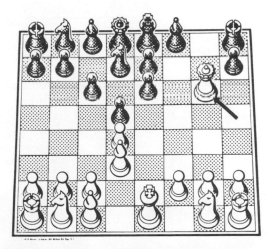

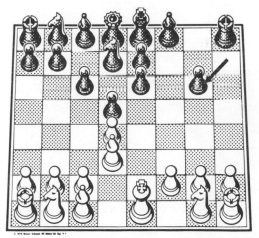

White plays **7 QxNPch!** This Queen sacrifice is spectacular, although the more obvious sacrifice of the Bishop by 7 BxPch would have the same effect.

Black plays **7 . . . PxQ,** a forced reply. Black now pays the penalty for having neglected his King's safety at move 5 with the faulty . . . PxP??

89

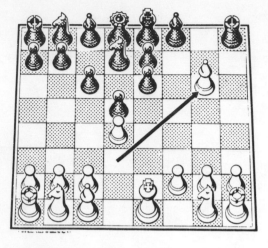

White plays **8 BxP mate,** a pleasing example of a brilliant sacrifice that leads to a spectacular mate.

The swiftness of Black's downfall is astonishing because the opening moves seem concerned with a purely strategic problem: the Pawn control of the center.

If Black had continued correctly (3 ... PxP and then 4 ... N—B3), he would have solved all his difficulties: control of the center, the beginning of correct development, and the problem of shielding his King from danger.

Instead, Black made two bad Knight moves and then opened a line to his King by capturing the advanced Pawn. Thereupon White's sacrifice of his Queen (or Bishop) was not too great a price for him to pay for achieving checkmate.